The Moral Priorities of Jesus

What Does Jesus Want From Us?

By Larry Harvey

*"Not everyone who says to me, 'Lord, Lord,'
will enter the kingdom of heaven,
but only the one who does the will
of my Father who is in heaven."*
- Jesus (Matthew 7:21)

*"Why do you call me, 'Lord, Lord,'
and do not do what I say?"*
- Jesus (Luke 6:46)

CONTENTS

PREFACE

a. The Gospels as History

If you wonder what I think about the historical records regarding Jesus, here's my position: In keeping with the results of strong recent scholarship I take the Gospel reporting about Jesus (in Matthew, Mark, Luke, and John) largely at face value. It is credible history, credibly presented, built on a broad base of eyewitness testimony.

b. Paying Attention to Jesus

You may not agree with my approach, but I hope you will agree it is worth considering what kind of Jesus shows up from such study. These are, after all, very early documents, and have had great influence throughout Western culture for two millennia.

Modern Christians often claim that they "believe in" Jesus, which implies paying close attention to him. This booklet may help us decide if they (we) are succeeding at that.

c. The Big Purpose of This Little Book

I'm not trying to answer all the arguments or cover all the bases. But shouldn't it be possible to put into two or three dozen pages the essentials of Jesus' approach to life? You'll have to decide if this comes near to succeeding at that. At any rate, the effort has impressed me more than ever with what an extraordinary person Jesus of Nazareth really was – and is.

INTRODUCTION: WHY WAS HE REJECTED?

Early in his career Jesus was often invited to speak in synagogue (comparable to church today). But it was not long before a person could be expelled from synagogue for being loyal to that same Jesus.

What happened? He obviously offended or frightened powerful people in both politics and religion. They, after all, are the ones who teamed up to get him first excluded, then executed.

The Bible indicates that his positions on good versus evil - what is moral and what is immoral - were a large part of the problem.

It makes you wonder. What did he teach that was so threatening to the powers that be? Why did he persist in such a dangerous direction? Would he get in trouble today with our political and religious leaders if he came with the same sort of teaching? After all, now as then, religion, politics, and economics are very big parts of life.

Seven themes in the moral teaching of Jesus are discussed in these short chapters. What were the moral priorities of Jesus? What does Christ-based Christian morality look like? Perhaps these short chapters can help answer these questions.

1 ○ JESUS' LOVE FOR GOD AND RELIGION

At first Jesus was attractive to religious people, which makes his later rejection by many leaders very interesting. But why did he look good to them at the beginning?

People saw Jesus as being devoted to God, the Scriptures, prayer, the Temple, and the synagogues - and he was - he talked and lived that way.

He was eager to discuss theology and Scripture with the most well-educated theologians of his day when he was only twelve years old, and they welcomed his interest and questions. As an adult Jesus often drew on the Jewish Scriptures; he often went apart by himself to pray; he was regularly in synagogue on Sabbath, wherever he was. He was recognized as a respectable religious teacher and was welcomed to teach in many synagogues in the early part of his career. When he went home to Nazareth he was invited to give the "sermon" there.

In his base city of Capernaum he was well known and perhaps even a recognized Rabbi in the synagogue. He was certainly invited and welcome to speak there. Jairus, "a ruler" of the synagogue, called on Jesus when his daughter was dying. A Roman military officer who financed their new synagogue held Jesus in high regard, and called on Jesus for help when his servant was sick.

In addition, there were supernatural affirmations of his goodness and spiritual quality. When he was baptized a "voice came from heaven: 'You are my Son, whom I love; with you I am well pleased'." Once when he was alone with three close followers, "a bright cloud enveloped them, and a voice from the cloud said, 'This is my Son, whom I love; with him I am well pleased. Listen to him!'" (Mark 1:11; Matthew 17:5)

Even at the end, when his highly placed enemies had determined to arrest him, they said - at least in public - "Teacher, we know you are a man of integrity" and "You do not show partiality but teach the way of God in accordance with truth." (Mark 12:14; Luke 20:21)

So here was a man whose private practice and public reputation both affirmed his complete devotion to God and to the religion of the Jews and their Scriptures.

HE HAD VERY CLEAR MORAL STANDARDS WHICH WERE
DERIVED FROM "THE LAW AND THE PROPHETS," ...
PROBLEMS AROSE BECAUSE THE CULTURAL PATTERNS
AND THE POWERFUL PEOPLE WERE NOT ACCUSTOMED
TO THOSE STANDARDS AND WERE UNWILLING TO
MOVE TOWARD THEM.

2 ○ JESUS INVERTED COMMON MORAL IDEAS

There was a problem. Jesus' moral doctrines seemed to many people to be way out of line - to the point of being dangerous.

a. Self-Satisfied Religion

In the Gospels Jesus does not mention homosexuality, and that was a time when it was more common in society than at many other times in history.

However, there is a strong tradition associating the city name of Sodom with homosexual behavior, holding that their homosexuality was so offensive to God that he destroyed that city.

Imagine how the good citizens of Capernaum felt when Jesus placed them below Sodom on the scale of moral goodness! "And you, Capernaum . . . it will be more bearable for Sodom on the day of judgment than for you." There is no mention of homosexual behavior in Capernaum, nor does Jesus mention sexual behavior of any sort in this complaint. The problem is, they will not deal with the plain fact that God is now active in their midst in very unusual ways. (Matthew 11:23,24)

Jesus indicated that their self-satisfied, impervious religion was much more deeply damaging and evil than whatever it was that caused Sodom's destruction. This is a major inversion of their system of moral evaluation, and a major insult - just as it would be if spoken to Christian believers today. His moral priorities were very different from those of his hearers. And he was willing to judge his hearers directly on the basis of their own behavior, not on whether they thought themselves superior to some other category of sinners.

b. Wealth, Power, Pomp – "The Powers That Be"

He did not pursue the wealth, power, and pomp of those who were "the important people" in his day, and he urged his hearers to follow his example. "The kings of the Gentiles lord it over them ... but you are not to be like that ... I am among you as one who serves." (Luke 22:25-30)

c. People Seen as "Less-Than"

He treated women with attention and respect - not the norm for his society. After his resurrection he chose to appear first to a woman - not to one of the men who dominated religion and society. His teaching about marriage and divorce greatly strengthened the wife's position in that society, and showed concern about just treatment of women by their husbands (and, by implication, vice versa).

He welcomed children, who were usually beneath the dignity of important people. He gave attention to the poor or powerless. He said, "Blessed are you poor" - but the poor do not often feel blessed; and those who are more powerful people think of themselves, not the poor, as the better off and enviable ones - the ones deserving God's blessing and favor. Some of them referred to the poor as "this mob that knows nothing of the (religious) law - there is a curse on them." Jesus did not talk like that. Jesus also said, "Blessed are you who hunger now," which brings up similar problems. (Luke 6:20,21; John 7:49)

He says he himself will one day judge the nations, but it will not be on the basis of their power, wealth, or prestigious place in the history books. He summarizes the judgment criteria like this: "Whatever you did for one of the least of these brothers of mine, you did for me." Attention to the little people, just treatment of the little people - this was not the practical morality of society's leaders in his day, and it has seldom if ever been so since. (Matthew 25:40,45)

Jesus never explicitly mentioned abortion or infanticide, though both were practiced in his day. But his concern for the little people, the powerless, the poor, and the exploited certainly has implications for this issue. (So also does the condemnation by the Prophets of infanticide as part of the worship of the idol Moloch.) Still, he does not mention it in the records we have.

d. What is Detestable?

What is detestable behavior? What are detestable achievements? Jesus said, "What is highly valued among men is detestable in God's sight." He was not speaking to the many Roman or Greek pagans who lived in Judea and Galilee, but to orthodox Jewish religious leaders; and he was talking about their own very religious and

Scripture-based values and habits. And he called them "detestable." His morality and spirituality were major problems for the popular moral and spiritual spokesmen. (Luke 16:15)

e. Courage and Respect

Once, when his enemies were trying to distract him by warning of Herod's interest in his activities, he in effect said, "Go tell that devious predator that I'll be on this road for the next three days doing powerful miracles he cannot even pretend to do; then I'll be in Jerusalem." Those are the words of a man not cowed by threats from the powerful.

He does not give much respect to the respected and the powerful. This is not moral relativism. He had very clear moral standards which were derived from "the Law and the Prophets," and he taught and lived by those standards. Problems arose because the cultural patterns and the powerful people were not accustomed to those standards and were unwilling to move toward them.

3 ○ JESUS AND RELIGION HAD A DIFFICULT RELATIONSHIP

The Pharisees were very serious about their faith. Although they were pompous about it, they were also good at it. Their religion — the Law of God — was their life. They were devoted, well-educated and highly disciplined.

And that is how they were seen by others. They set a very strict standard for religious holiness and had a reputation in general for practicing what they preached. And they were visible — recognizable in the streets by their distinctive attire and behavior. Because of their religious education, discipline and visibility, they often had prominent positions in the weekly synagogue meetings, sitting up front, reciting the many prayers or reading or commenting on Scripture.

a. Complaints About Religious Leaders

But this teacher Jesus — who was also highly respected for his goodness and for being serious about God and Scripture — this Jesus often spoke of them in public with contempt, withering scorn and condemnation.

For example, in the famous "Sermon on the Mount," Jesus speaks of his nation's holy writings ("the Law and the Prophets"), and of how important they are. Then he mentions the Pharisees. You might expect him to say "We need to listen to them. They are completely devoted to the Law and the Prophets, and are the standard of righteousness."

In fact he said, "unless your righteousness surpasses that of the Pharisees . . . you will certainly not enter the kingdom of heaven." This is a profound inversion of established religious morality. The experts and leaders in religion are not, morally or spiritually, even up to the bare minimum that God requires. (Matthew 5:20)

He was known to accept invitations to eat in the houses of Pharisees (an indication that he met at least some of their technical standards of righteousness), and then take the occasion to make the event difficult by energetically critiquing their religious practices in front of the other guests.

On one such occasion (a Sabbath day on which the holy could do no "work" - and healing the sick was regarded as work), Jesus was apparently being set up. "He was being carefully watched. There in front of him was a man suffering from dropsy." Jesus did not ignore the man, nor did he heal him later so as to avoid giving offense. He confronted the Pharisee's religious standards directly. "Is it lawful to heal on the Sabbath or not?" No answer. "So taking hold of the man he healed him and sent him away." (Luke 14:1-6)

b. Some Very Serious Charges

One time a Pharisee-host "was surprised" that Jesus bypassed the ritual hand-washing before going to the table. In response, Jesus launched into a strong series of complaints - insults in fact - against Pharisaic religion and morality. "You Pharisees clean the outside . . . but inside you are full of greed and wickedness." "Woe to you . . .

you neglect justice and the love of God." These are very serious charges.

There are six repetitions of "woe to you" in this short speech. This is a dumbfounding reversal of values. Here's the new, popular teacher of religion vigorously attacking the established holy men of his culture. Some were sure his enthusiasm and arrogance had caused him to corrupt true morality. No wonder the next comment is, "the Pharisees and teachers of the law began to oppose him fiercely." (Luke 11:37-53)

When his followers wondered, "Do you know that the Pharisees were offended?" he responded, "Leave them; they are blind guides." (Matthew 15:12-14)

He often publicly applied the word "hypocrite" to these - and other - leaders in his religion. It means "actor" or "pretender." His behavior would be comparable to standing outside churches or other religious establishments today, calling out to the pastor, preacher, priest or other leader, "You are a fraud! You say to do one thing, but you yourself are practicing the opposite!" Or, "You fakes! You do look good on the outside, but inside you are utterly corrupt."

c. Liberals and Conservatives

And let us not imagine that he was attacking the religious liberals in defense of the conservative positions. In important ways the Pharisees were the cultural and religious conservatives.

But Jesus also applied this kind of deep moral criticism to people prominent across the spectrum of religious, cultural and political life - "the chief priests," "the teachers of the law," "the Sadducees", "that fox" Herod, etc. He was willing to point out the obvious, in public, for the benefit of those who did not recognize it.

It earned him enemies.

d. His Own Solid Reputation

He was not a crank or a sociopath. He did it because he believed their morals were clearly wrong in extremely important ways. Remember, he himself had a solid reputation as a great teacher sent from God, a man devoted to God, to Scripture, prayer, the Temple and the synagogues.

Thus Jesus brought together in one integrated personality things that seemed then and seem to many of us today to be polar opposites - profound religious insight and moral power on the one hand, with explicit rejection of much of the established practice of religion on the other. He was publicly at odds with large and very important aspects of the culture of his own people. And the egos he offended belonged to people powerful enough to bring the whole power of the state to bear against him - which is just what they eventually did.

4 ○JESUS LOVED ORDINARY PEOPLE

Jesus was regularly seen at synagogue, and sometimes in the houses of the most important and respected people. But he was also regularly in the company of the "sinners" (the "bad" people of his day, those looked down on), fairly often in their houses or at their parties.

Jesus seemed to have a special attraction for the tax-gatherers who took the people's money for the hated Roman occupation. Those whose lives were sexually immoral - sometimes by their employment - gravitated to him. Jesus was quite comfortable at some parties and celebrations that were way out of line by the holy standards of the synagogues or the Pharisees.

When he was called to account for these facts he was not apologetic, but defended himself with no hint of regret or confusion.

And for all these people - in all their different categories of significance or insignificance, power or powerlessness, holiness or unholiness - he felt an obvious tenderness and concern, and a certain level of identification.

He truly saw the crowds that followed him. He was "moved with compassion," and saw them as "harassed and helpless". They were!

Signs of the Roman military occupation were all around. There was always reason to fear the secret police and spies of Herod's brutal regime. Tax farmers were everywhere, and the poorest carried a heavy load of taxation. Pharisees and other religionists condemned and despised whatever efforts "lesser" people made toward God or religion. (Matthew 9:36)

The only ones advocating for "ordinary people" against the religious, economic, and political powers were political radicals devoted to revolution or violence. Jesus refused to go that route. But he also refused to stay out of sight or keep quiet. He refused to ignore the real situation of so many of the people around him.

He actually loved these ordinary people. He served them directly with attention, physical and spiritual healing, with teaching they were hungry for, with forgiveness, and sometimes with lunch. He served them indirectly by regularly challenging the powerful persons who harassed them and kept them helpless. He also served them indirectly by recruiting them to serve each other.

It is interesting to observe that his harsher sayings were directed at religious authorities, sometimes at the wealthy, occasionally at the politically powerful, but almost never at the bulk of the population.

In the Gospel records, he never spoke explicitly against homosexual behavior. He never joined "the church people" of his day when they tried to stir up action against prostitutes, tax-gatherers, or people caught violating marriage vows. He attended parties and celebrations that the religious leaders thought sinful. He did not advocate that Temple or other religious authorities take over the government. He never accused the poor of causing their own poverty. He associated with a wide range of people. His values were not normal religious values! But he was very serious about them.

HE NEVER HONORED THE RICH FOR THEIR SUCCESS. HE NEVER ENCOURAGED THE WEALTHY TO LIGHTEN THEIR SOCIAL OBLIGATIONS, NOR DID HE GIVE THEM MUCH CREDIT FOR THEIR DONATIONS TO THE TEMPLE. HE SINGLED OUT FOR HONOR A POOR WIDOW (QUITE POSSIBLY A SINGLE MOTHER) WHO GAVE ALMOST NOTHING.

5 ○ TO JESUS, ECONOMICS AND EXPLOITATION WERE MORAL ISSUES

Jesus did not major on economic issues, but he certainly did not avoid them. In fact he might have agreed with the idea expressed earlier by Plato that every city is two cities, one of the rich, one of the poor, and that they are not working together for each other's good. (Plato said, "These are at war with one another.")

Jesus said, "Watch out for the teachers of the law. They like to walk around in flowing robes and be greeted in the market places and have the most important seats in the synagogues and the places of honor at banquets. They devour widows' houses and for a show make lengthy prayers. Such men will be punished most severely." (Mark 12:36-40) Among these "church" leaders we find long faces, long robes, long prayers, long fingers - and long punishment.

No doubt the foreclosures on those widows' houses were entirely legal. These men were making astute investments and reaping the just rewards of their foresight and willingness to put their capital at risk. It was unfortunate, but not their fault, that some women do not fulfill their financial obligations.

But in the moral vision of Jesus it looked very different. "Such men will be punished most severely."

However he never said it is wrong to be wealthy. When the apparently corrupt tax-farmer Zaccheus promised to refund any illegitimate gain he had taken (plus considerable interest - "four times the amount"!), and to disperse half of his wealth to the poor, Jesus said, "Today salvation has come to this house." He did not ask the tax man to get rid of all his wealth, nor did he require a change of employment. (Luke 9:1-10)

But he did ask another wealthy man to give away everything. Then he responded to his followers' amazement with two observations. First, "How hard it is for a rich man to enter the kingdom of God." Second, "What is impossible with men is possible with God." (Luke 18:24-27)

He never honored the rich for their success. He never encouraged the wealthy to lighten their social obligations, nor did he give them much credit for their donations to the Temple. He singled out for honor a poor widow (quite possibly a single mother) who gave almost nothing.

He told a story of a rich man who died and went to a place of torment while the poor man who lay in the street by his gate went to a place of comfort.

Another time a rich farmer is called "You fool" because he was unable to value anything, not even God, above his increasing wealth. (Luke 16:19; 12:20)

We cannot avoid the idea that to Jesus' way of thinking wealth does not correlate well with eternal blessedness.

These are serious issues in today's America, and today's world, as they have been in every land in every century. Not surprisingly, they were serious issues in the mind of Jesus

IF THERE IS EVIL (OR GOOD) LURKING WITHIN, IT IS
SOBERING TO CONSIDER THIS: JESUS HAS THE EFFECT
OF MAKING THE INVISIBLE OBVIOUS. BECAUSE OF HIM,
"THE THOUGHTS OF MANY HEARTS WILL BE REVEALED."

6 ○ FOR JESUS, THE INVISIBLE IS ALWAYS MORE IMPORTANT

He would surely have agreed with the words of Paul written maybe twenty years later: "What is seen is temporary, but what is unseen is eternal." He got more specific, teaching that if your gains are only in the visible realm, they are meaningless. "What good will it be for a man if he gains the whole world (visible gain), yet forfeits his soul (invisible loss)?" (2 Corinthians 4:18; Matthew 6:22)

He spoke often of "the kingdom of God" and the "kingdom of heaven," and his earliest preaching is summarized as "Repent, for the kingdom of God is near." At that time it was difficult to interpret his kingdom talk without visualizing secret police, military power, fortresses, palaces, vast wealth accumulations, and pomp and circumstance. (Mark 1:15; Matthew 4:17)

But those things were never apparent around Jesus - neither before his execution, nor after his resurrection. If there was a kingdom, it wasn't very visible. If he had the key place in it, that was not demonstrated by the symbols of authority - wealth and power - that people expected from kings. If he had authority, it was not displayed or enforced by laws, police, courts, soldiers, or prisons.

"Nor will people say, 'Here it (the kingdom of God) is,' or 'There it is,' because the kingdom of God is within (or among) you." He really believed the Kingdom was already there! (Luke 17:21)

Kingdoms establish (and enforce) the moral environment of their societies. We would particularly expect the Kingdom of God to do so. If somehow the Kingdom of God is truly present, it is an invisible power that can establish a new moral (and physical) environment. Jesus believed in this invisible kingdom as the most important moral reality.

Also, he liked to tell the people to not be afraid, to not worry. He knew as well as they that there was much good reason for worry. But he looked beyond that to greater, invisible realities both within a person's own life, and in the kingdom of God. He's not avoiding the facts of life; he believes he knows the greater, more powerful and more significant facts within world history, and within individual lives.

He saw the importance of the invisible "inner" part of being a human individual. "Nothing that enters a man from the outside can make him unclean … what comes out of a man is what makes him unclean." Then follows a powerful list of morally wrong behaviors (including "thoughts"!) "For from within, out of men's hearts, come evil thoughts, sexual immorality, theft, murder, adultery, greed, malice, deceit, lewdness, envy, slander, arrogance and folly. All these evils come from inside and make a man unclean." (Mark 7:20-23)

Obviously Jesus is taking a stand against all these things. That is, he's not saying these behaviors are tolerable if only your heart is in the right place.

But the point here is that these evil behaviors have roots. Those invisible roots in the human heart are the power behind evil behavior in the physical world, at whatever level.

If there is evil (or good) lurking within, it is sobering to consider this: Jesus has the effect of making the invisible obvious. Because of him, "the thoughts of many hearts will be revealed." "There is nothing concealed that will not be disclosed, or hidden that will not be made known." (Luke 2:35; Matthew 10:26)

According to Jesus, the invisible - both inside of each of us, and in the world at large - is where the moral powers have their home, and there lies the source of human action.

7 ○ DID JESUS HAVE AN EGO PROBLEM?

People spoke very highly of Jesus, often even calling him "Lord." Instead of resisting that high praise, he pressed them to practice what it implied. "Why do you call me 'Lord, Lord,' but do not do the things that I say?" (Luke 6:46)

This brings up a moral emphasis in the teachings of Jesus that can seem strange in our world. He thought extremely highly of himself - in terms of the value of his teaching, and in terms of his importance to the future welfare of individuals and even of the whole of world history. Strange that may be, but it is clearly an issue of values, of morality.

It's interesting that he did not spend a lot of time talking about this, and was not what we might call "touchy" about it. He seemed to just assume it; and occasionally, when it was appropriate to the issue at hand, he spoke clearly about this value and its implications.

For example, this young man (32 or 33) assumed that he was entirely capable of protecting and "gathering" that great city of Jerusalem, and was deeply saddened that they did not respond to his invitation. He wept about it, "Because you did not recognize the time of God's coming." "O Jerusalem, Jerusalem . . . how often I have longed to gather your children together." Then he makes the stunningly arrogant claim, "You will not see me again until you say, 'Blessed is he who comes in the name of the Lord.'" (Luke 19:41-44; Luke 13:34-35)

He told a story in which he was the one sent by God to take possession of the nation, presenting himself as "the [corner-] stone the builders rejected." The religious leaders of the nation "knew he had spoken this parable against them." (Luke 20:9-19)

He was not reluctant to apply that same sort of thinking at the personal level. He said, "I am the gate for the sheep" (for the people). When asked, "How can we know the way?" he answered, "I am the way," and "if you really knew me, you would know my Father as well." (John 10:7; 14:5-7)

He said that he himself will be the one, in a future time of his own power and glory, to "reward each person according to what he has done," and to judge "the nations." (Matthew 16:27; 25:31-32)

This ego-centrism, or inflated self-image, is of staggering proportions!

But morality and ethics are about higher and lower values, so this also must be seen as a persistent part of the moral teachings of Jesus, a part that has been consistently recognized down through subsequent history. It is not something to imitate — unless we think we are truly on a par with this man and can justly make the same claims and offers that he made. But we must consider it as we try to understand and relate to the morals and the moral impact he has had throughout history.

8 ○ HOW CAN WE "BELIEVE IN" THIS JESUS?

a. The Gospels Insist - We Need to Believe in Him

To all who did receive him, to those who believed in his name, he gave the right to become children of God (John 1:12)

For God so loved the world that he gave his one and only Son, that whoever believes in him shall not perish but have eternal life. (John 3:16)

How can you believe since you accept glory from one another but do not seek the glory that comes from the only God? (John 5:44)

Jesus heard that they had thrown him out, and when he found him, he said, "Do you believe in the Son of Man?"

"Who is he, sir?" the man asked. "Tell me so that I may believe in him."

Jesus said, "You have now seen him; in fact, he is the one speaking with you."

Then the man said, "Lord, I believe," and he worshiped him. (John 9:35-38)

Jesus performed many other signs in the presence of his disciples, which are not recorded in this book. But these are written that you may believe that Jesus is the Messiah, the Son of God, and that by believing you may have life in his name. (John 20:30,31)

b. That is a Very Deep and Demanding Thing

It often shows as

- strong respect for him,
- fascination with his character and personality,
- humility before his wisdom and love,
- an attitude of thorough honest self-aware confession before his honesty, justice, and kindness
- longing to follow his teaching and wisdom,
- commitment to shape our lives under his authority,
- willingness to listen to him over self-promoting, self-aggrandizing religious leaders and groups,
- desire to serve the people in our world whom he is concerned to serve.

It is a very big thing – which is what we would expect if Jesus really is who and what we say he is.

c. Today's Watered-Down Version

Unfortunately that requirement has been redefined in modern American Christian circles. It is now possible to imagine that we believe in Jesus when in fact we accord him a very small, in some cases almost nonexistent, level of respect and attention.

That doesn't work. He is smarter than that, and expects us to be too.

Today church leaders usually do not ask us to surrender our lives to the teaching and wisdom and guidance of this Great One, Jesus. We don't hear much, if anything, about what his teaching is, or what his actual guidance for our lives would be. How is that respectful?

They may, and often do, ask us to surrender our lives (or at least our money) to them or to their organizations. And, of course, we do hear about a certain few "sins" that happen to be the ones our groups choose to talk about most. They also usually happen to be ones that Jesus did not emphasize or even mention. Also, they don't appear publicly very often in our contemporary American Christian circles. How convenient is that?

A Common Prayer: Today we are just asked to acknowledge something about who we think Jesus is. And we are usually asked to make a simple statement that we are sinners and need forgiveness (with no sins explicitly mentioned). These modern belief-requirements often come together in a short prayer something like "Jesus, I acknowledge you as Lord. I admit that I am a sinner and need your forgiveness. I invite you into my life as Lord and Savior."

Adolf Hitler, in his public speeches to the German people in the 1930's, referred to Jesus as "my Lord and Savior Jesus Christ." Because he said things like that, many "German Christians" gave their allegiance to him as their "Christian" leader. They were wrong.

d. Actually Believe in Him

Jesus himself said, "Why do you call me 'Lord, Lord' but do not do what I say?" Now that's the right question! "Why?" indeed!

> "There is absolutely nothing in what Jesus himself or his early followers taught that suggests you can decide just to enjoy forgiveness at Jesus's expense and have nothing more to do with him." - Dallas Willard (The Great Omission, p13)

You see, to believe in the Lord Jesus, as the Bible presents the idea over and over – and as history shows our English word "believe" to actually mean – is to love, to deeply admire, to cling to as a source of wisdom and truth and guidance and care. To believe in Jesus has a very strong connection to what Jesus called the greatest commandment – to love God with all your being. It is a very high standard.

e. It's Free - Anybody Can Do It

And it merits no special credit; it's the most obvious, elementary thing that needs doing in human life. It gives no bragging rights whatsoever.

But it's not imaginary; it is the most basic, gut-level reality and necessity. Nothing matters more.

f. Can You Believe?

How can you believe in him if you don't care what he thinks?

Can you believe in him if, when you get down to it, you really don't want to know about or invest in the things that he cares most about?

Can you believe in him if you have no interest in living in a way that is pleasing to him?

Can you believe in him if you are unwilling to commit to learning him and to following his values and priorities?

Can you believe in him if being approved of by your friends or your peers is going to have more influence in your decisions and lifestyle than he himself?

Can you believe in him if you don't want to live in a world structured according to his values and preferences? That, after all, is what the new world he is bringing will be.

Can you believe in him if you love money or status more than you love him?

Can you believe if you love being right, in your own opinion, more than you love being corrected by him, learning from him and living his loving, serving, welcoming priorities in this damaged world?

It matters a great deal what Jesus wants – what his moral priorities are – because, after all, what he loves and values – that's a big part of who he is. If we don't accept those things, then we don't accept him. And if we don't accept him - don't even really like him - how dare we say we believe in him?

g. A Very Short Assignment:

If you were to write or speak a statement to Jesus making explicit your truly believing in him – in light of the things you just read - what might it say? What would you want it to say? What do you need to think through? Dare you write it out? He is gracious – if you need to edit it in days to come as your insight increases, he understands that. I say, give it a try.

Conclusion

a. Here Was a Real Man

Here was a man of integrity - a man who said it as he saw it, and looked carefully, honestly and with profound moral insight in order to see it right.

Here was a man thoroughly committed to know and justly interpret God and the Scriptures.

Here was a man who truly loved God with all his being.

Here was a man not corrupted by the natural human hungers for pleasure, or for status or wealth, or for the approval of those who had the status and wealth.

Here was a man who loved people, all the time, everywhere, and in the concrete, not only as abstractions.

b. The Intersect of Money, Power, and Religion

A major issue in his teaching, especially in terms of its impact on his ministry and his life, is the problem of the complex intersection between money, power, and religion. The Pharisees were in some ways very conservative socially, but "the Pharisees loved money." The Sadducees were traditional in their religious emphases, but were very much in love with political and governmental power. Essenes and other fringe "holiness" groups were largely irrelevant to the real lives of ordinary people, and to true holiness as well. Zealots were concerned about justice and mistreatment of the nation, but they were willing to depend on violence. Herod and Pilate, with Rome standing behind them, provided a measure of political and military stability, but were corrupt in every way.

c. His Independence

Whatever Jesus said or did would put him into conflict with two or three factions, or with all of them. That would likely be the case today, as well. Jesus had to take a new road; he had to make the road. In fact, near the end, he said he was the road.

So which of all those power centers would approve of that? And how about us? Do WE want this Jesus, the real one?

d. He Asks Us to be His Witnesses

Writing this summary of the moral priorities of Jesus has been a deep pleasure, and a humbling one. There is so much there. In the presence of a character like this, and an authority like his, the idea of trying to summarize it all in black and white seems arrogant. But he asks us to bear witness to him, and this is one way to do that. It is an honor.

e. How Will You Remember?

If this little book is helpful it's probably worth reading again – and doing some underlining, or making of notes in the margins. If these things are true, we need to increase our awareness of Jesus, not let it fade away.

CHANGED
PRIORITIES
AHEAD

www.ingramcontent.com/pod-product-compliance
Lightning Source LLC
Chambersburg PA
CBHW021122020426
42331CB00004B/581